Awful Gestures

Chapbooks by the author

Gypsy
Bad Girls

Awful Gestures

Adrienne Weiss

INSOMNIAC PRESS

Edited by Lynn Crosbie
Copy-edited by Catherine Jenkins
Designed by Mike O'Connor

National Library of Canada Cataloguing in Publication Data

Weiss, Adrienne, 1973–
     Awful Gestures: poems

ISBN 1-894663-12-8

I. Title.

PS8595.E488A9 2001   C811'.54 C2001-902147-X
PR9199.3.W3994A9 2001

The publisher and the author gratefully acknowledges the sup-
port of the Canada Council, the Ontario Arts Council and
Department of Canadian Heritage through the Book Publishing
Industry Development Program.

Printed and bound in Canada

Insomniac Press, 192 Spadina Avenue, Suite 403,
Toronto, Ontario, Canada, M5T 2C2
www.insomniacpress.com

THE CANADA COUNCIL | LE CONSEIL DES ARTS
FOR THE ARTS | DU CANADA
SINCE 1957 | DEPUIS 1957

ONTARIO ARTS COUNCIL
CONSEIL DES ARTS DE L'ONTARIO

For my father, Ralph—
with love and respect reaching beyond any star

Acknowledgements

I'd like to thank Lynn Crosbie a thousand times—for everything.

I'd like to thank Carleton Wilson for showing me what strength is, and for ordering these poems with care.

I'd like to thank Mary Crosbie for her friendship and generous heart.

I'd like to thank Nushik Narsis for being a constant inspiration.

I'd like to thank Andy Boorman for sharing his spirit with me.

I'd like to thank Sherwin Tjia for helping me think of the perfect title.

I'd like to thank the Insomniacs: Mike O'Connor, Richard Almonte and Jan Barbieri.

I'd like to thank the following for their encouraging advice: James Arthur, Kevin Connolly, Lynnette D'anna, Michael Holmes, A.F. Moritz, Stuart Ross and Paul Vermeersch.

Thank you to the Algonquin SquareTable who work-shopped many of the poems here: James, Ed Baranosky, Rachel Bokhout, Jennifer Bronson, Carolyn Clink, David Clink, Raymond Gallardo, Adam Getty, Kristi-ly Green, Mici Gold, Ray Hsu,

Sandra Kasturi, Caroline Li, Susan Manchester, Lisa O'Leary, Al, Dana Snell, Souvankham Thammavongsa, Susan Vickberg, Myna Wallin and Carleton.

Thanks to the following for their support: Janet Bailey, Julie Bot, Dawn Calleja, Jeanie Calleja, Anne Cox, Steve Cox, Gabriela Hahn, Brad Hart, Tara McCallan, Sharon Moon, Noam Rosen, Martha Solomon and Krista Weiss.

Finally, thanks to my family—especially Mum.

*I know how furiously
your heart is beating.*
—Wallace Stevens

Rain is no ordinary miracle

Rain is no
ordinary miracle. On
the streets, diner and
club lights make a
traffic jam of wet
halos. Waiting on a
streetcar, a heart
catches fire; is
quickly squelched by
neon drizzle, a drunk's
muttering. Stray notes
merge, *in the days when
we went gipsying,
a long time ago*, a pull to
surrender, loneliness
beats. The streetcar
stumbles through this
beauty to illusion,
devouring its
passengers.

Subterranean

Darkness here is permanent. Time a layer of abandoned rails. I crawl into the vacancy of this landscape, listening for you, reminded of the broken expanse of dreams. And in that state of waking, wide-eyed, you come out, stumbling. Somehow leaving fits, the love you have for the idea of it. I take your finger and trace an outline from the seams of split skin to the muscle of my heart breeding daisies, wild and unassuming. I take you out of the frozen soil, its treeless wake. And offer you the stories of my country.

Scar

I bring you my scars. In your
hand they stretch and embrace
rivets of skin. This design of me,
a frozen, cracked stream; my
lifeblood's irrigation system.

And flying on spent wings, coiling
the edge of knuckle, wrist, they
lead to the centre of things. The
calloused extension of palm that
crumbles to fall, light as a flutter

in the chest. Its heart, clothed and
textured in gingham where I once held
you, cocooned in fresh starch. Or spread
the length of my arms, when I folded
then tucked you, neat. Away.

But quietly, a butterfly is rustling,
breaking my skin where the veins
intersect a blue course. And scarring
the inner lining where you pin me, still.

A Pretty Mistake

I shall never get you put together entirely,
Pieced, glued, and properly jointed.

— Sylvia Plath

You have taken too long to leave and it's
much too hard to breathe in here, with each

feeling palpable and you didn't mean to knock
the glass and spill your wordless heart.

And you don't want his cruel insomnia, a body
punishing you, this awkward tenderness he

shows. And you don't know why the sun is not
comforting, why you are not really living, or

why he is in sensual disarray, mass-produced
and sick. And you have heard him cry enough

about dreams that don't translate into reality,
about why he's not full, all body, all

darkness; but mostly that you are scared of
his desire. And you don't like whispering, it's

too much like he never wanted you to hear
him, or a chill you can't evade. And you can't

recall why you couldn't ever say: *wash*

me in you, every part, starting with your

tears, but you couldn't and watch love wake
fast to grey rain, slip into a colour and fall

into a broken light; his heart a diamond
shard on the floor and your cut hand a pretty

mistake. You come out of the room with
these dreams fresh and gushing. Shuffling,

tired, you take a place in the morning,
amid the apartment's other rooted

artifacts. And just when you've settled, he
enters, but not from the bedroom and you're

suddenly not sure where he's come from. But
he's there looking at you and you are shocked

and can only offer the dreams bleeding from
your hand.

Stand Behind the Yellow Line

I

The wait to catch a rush-hour
subway gives me time to apply
ideas with a #6 Mac liner brush;
its tip softened by tongue, a
painted dialogue: *all things are
artificiall, for Nature is the Art of
God* and that takes work. I purse
my lips, dab Lipglass, consider it
a shining tribute to better beauty
as I stand behind the yellow line.

II

Bodies juggle toward work and
Toronto resembles a warehouse,
antique with its ruined facade,
craggy rooftop. Split open are
billboard choir girls who sing to
the air, the cracked flimsiness of
the expressway. Birds marvel at
entering and falter with leaving,
black flutter against no Order.

And down my throat, a dream.
Mind the gaps—I'm just
talking.

Queen Bee

She contemplates the made-up
mess of her face and

wonders that the room
didn't notice her
absence or presence, that

she didn't recognize any other way
out but
a quick exit and on

the subway
speculates change is sudden.
Knowing that's false,
passing each stop.
It's a progression,
with each realization,
mutter and mistake that

dangles from her mouth brimming
with sting. And her heart
slips,
reckless to speak but

throbs stupidly, wants the next
moment,
a rush to now—

she sees she is nothing but
a Queen Bee
flitting in a diamanté blouse,
gorging on her arrogant,
honey-young

self.

Sweetheart Roland

for Julie Bot

Sweetheart Roland starts
back toward the village,
over the macadam. Already
set, a rose, I wait out the
season. Petals uncurl,
unsmiling, to reveal beryl,

remains of love. It is because
of the sting of space between,
heart in diastolic motion, with
spring stealth that I start back,
furtive; another way.

Dead Flies

for Gabriela Hahn

Gabriela scourges the floor, 10:15 a.m.
I tiptoe round her, a cloudy light head of
chemical lemon.

Bright, spanning windows wash us in
grey: St. Clair's treetops, a brown
mass with their knifed fingers.

There's coffee. Everything she says
is an announcement to which I nod and
am glad she's thought of.

I sip and sit with ivy, cacti and rose
geraniums; she sighs, changing the
colour of the room.

I watch her work, think of chasing
answers. Still in a dream confusion,
remembering my fears, sipping,

burning tongue. And living in shadows,
a life already lived before, the previous
tenant; her dates and memories marked

in the wall, choice of paper, where
portraits hung and at night I hear her
typing out last words, as if it were the

day before she died. (Quiet, unobtrusive,
Gabriela grinds at the surface). In another
time I too must've died, die every day in

passing, in space, empty then full then dark.
There is a startled grunt: *Another one. I
picked one up yesterday; it must've*

suffocated on geranium odour. She
sweeps the fifth dead fly this week and I
settle again, dust.

Road Kill:
leaving you in a suburban restaurant

It was the unreality of the room
that led to thoughts of bigger
things, of somewhere else, like
Toronto—an exotic idea. I
swirled liquid chocolate with
my fork and calmed our heat
with a strawberry fan as you talked. I
was distracted by the cook's fine
armour; like a modern culinary
Augustus, he cocked his ridiculous
helmet, bloodstained from
morning slaughter. And my
concocted life went on in its dull
way of raging; our routine became
manipulation, our bodies diligent
till my mind dismembered and
you... were... still... talking...
Desperate, dirty fingers biding
time, slipped and were cut by a
steak knife. Myself sliced open
like watermelon, shocked;
my tight nerve endings
drumming. I imagined a crow
picked at a squirrel in a milky
gutter somewhere. A spider
capturing a fly and the smell of
blood when it hits oxygen—
lovely like red wine. You were
sweet with embarrassment.
Across the room a woman

stared at my bloody thumb. Her
mouth heavy, blowing tears of
smoke, her tongue licking her
fermented lips. But it was you
who left wounded and I've often
wondered about the scar, what
you told those who noticed the
strange split in your palm that
travels the lifeline and circles
your thin wrist. You left me there,
a stain on linen, unfinished design,
wondering about bigger things,
being somewhere else, like exotic
Toronto, and what animal would
sniff at my thumb, eager for a taste.

I watch you, real hard

I watch you, real hard.
You might be *animal*.
And want to be preyed upon.
For this, I think *touch you*.
You grunt when I pull a fist
out of your gut.

Your blood tells me you'll taste good.

Pop Art

They pull into Esso, the car tired of coughing.
102.1 blaring, yet noiseless to Karen's pop ears.
Jim is surprised he has no money and prods

for her Royal Bank client card, the code.
But she is withdrawn, the money gone, an
overdraft. It is easy to survey him from the

passenger seat: his frame black against flashing
movie poster lights and BAR OPEN at Rebecca and
Lakeshore Dr. He doesn't bother checking for his

gas card, asks for cash. But she strays her eyes
beyond him and the Supervideo. Overhead, evening
flutters to a close and she is not yet sure of him.

I would like it if the sky were always like this,
she said to Jim out the window, not having heard
his hesitation, erratic breath. She becomes idle and

fiddles with the vanity mirror, her dragonfly
hairpins. Karen thinks how pretty her hair looks,
purple and yellow glitter at the sides, just above

the ears and Jim pokes again for money. Deposited,
she hands him a ten and their transaction is com-
plete.

Timeless

for Jeanie Calleja

The drive into Havelock anticipates a lazy
cottage, hard backs floating on the brown
lake and girls anorexic with talk.

All of us want a turn at spinning in the tire,
to make waves and push each other out.
All of us want to sit on the shore's rock face,

slide down its slick mossy skull and grapple
with the water's hands. Mostly we want to
discover we are timeless.

A Heart Like Yours

Someday, he said, *I'll have a heart
like yours in my arms.* Dirt-stained,
hunk of root still clinging. It'll wriggle

and cry for earth, calloused raw and
not pink but blue. *I will not have had
time to disinfect it.*

With a free hand he'll tickle its arterial
wrists. Breathing will be easier, your
heart muscle contracting, regular in his

hold. You'll call him a *murderer*, but how
could you understand the details of killing,
of dead bees crackling underfoot, hissing

climbers, breaths catching on corroded
shards of igneous rock. You'll stand at the
edge, perpetually teetering between love and

hate for him. He'll say *that is what it means
to have faith*, but you'll misinterpret these
granite words pounding with porphyritic

glitter. The particular impulses of a heart,
like yours.

Itinerant Job

with thanks to A.F. Moritz

Drawn *the steep and thorny way*
to heaven I wander the heart of
its brusque landscape, His houses of
clay; deep crevasses where
prisoners of love dig.

I resist their graves marked by
lavender stones and flowers strewn
like garbage. With burning feet I
near morning's rocky horizon arm,
am stung by his indifferent

reception. But I won't ever mistake
His face, curling from the sun, cold
as jade and culpable. And in my
travel log, He is dated and fixed in
these words I smudge to you on a postcard.

Unwavering, linoleum rain pelts on

Unwavering, linoleum rain pelts on
weekend travellers in tin boxes. I think
of nothing but keeping my eyes open,
high gas prices, smell of Tim Hortons,
grainy music and a sun that darkens on me.
I'm on a wedding trip for an old friend, at
the church where I became a Girl Guide.

This drive cleans you from my skin. I still
wonder to know you and lean into any
offering you make. With a voice that talks
itself into an August heat, is held like glass.
I am suspended by you as I make the tense
exit, wanting to save you when you fall,
because you will fall

and I won't be ready.

A Deep Shade of Remedy

The weary, listening street
answers a bird bathing in

dirt with bread. Answers me
with an abrupt run into you.

I reach and am not reached for.
Your impatient hands don't

see the roses I carry are
burning my flesh. And what's

five years, three weeks, the
hour we first met. You reached

and I would not be reached for.
An old desire grieves; the bird

caught in a dirt tornado grieves.
Your blind hand clasps mine,

tremulous; the hour we first met
roses never burnt in our flesh—

now your palms are red-petal ash;
our hands, a deep shade of remedy.

Beyond the Flurry

I've manufactured you,
an illusion that enters me
like absinthe, swarms me
like a gale till I suffocate.

I'm not sure I'm being honest,
can't think to feel; can't be
with you and be separate,
unknown.

I just want time to fill itself
with gossamer song, just fill
and fill till I see beyond the
flurry of our limbs,

the certain weight of you.

Stay

for D.A.

Do you want to stay your hand
whispered, slipping through an
undulating spread of ash, dark hair.

That night I dragged in the snow
like a trail of broken pearls; I fell
against your weary heart, monotheistic.

There was a finality to that morning,
and then, with the ones that followed—
I was always leaving you, naked and smooth,
to burn in the sheets—

I remember I watched you lie there,
fumbling to put the necklace back together,
wanting to be Jesus. And I took care to
make the bed less empty.

Dextrarum Junctio
(The Joining of Right Hands)

Legs scissor, open and
close for you. Close when
you are through.

Now you are through.
Legs close and
leak. The lure of you soft.

Against the
tree, a voice repeats
push push

Legs spread,
membrane bursts,
12:35 a.m. and pissing blood
into the toilet,

I am in the warm sea of you.

Careful Where You Tread

I wait between bruises, the
pressure of hand. All beauty is
the same to you and I must push
to change. Through a June fog,
there is my surprise at the end.
Of the raw, tumbling mornings
of you. I pull to breathe and am
careful where the blood treads.

In my heat you disappear

In my heat you disappear
where you are and smoke
makes a sign in the air. A
familiar ease I try to rest in.
Consider the name of. And
lingering, vanishing within
an armoury of pink skin, a
final kiss grasps for the next
heartbeat

but whose pulse is this
    whose breath or sigh
catches the moment I have lost you,
      and can I claim the way you move,
        can I sound, rhythm
          you,
          can I stir you into

grace

Night Comes For Sleep
—Laila ba l'sheina

I didn't wake to the firecrackers,
though breathing in bed was hard.

I dreamed you, lovely like untouched
water and the deep spread of your

voice, drowning sleep. I dreamed you
opening walls and startling the cold out

of me.

But I didn't wake to the firecrackers,
though breathing in bed was hard.

I saw patios struggling to stay open
and city streets ruined with anger; you

opening the walls and startling the cold
out of me—*you*—lovely like

untouched water—the deep spread of
possession, I struggled to stay open

for you—

but breathing in bed was hard,
without you—

and I didn't wake to the firecrackers.
I don't wake anymore; am left

dreaming of your voice, ruined with anger,
a startling pulse of drowning words.

The Myth of Tantalus

Agitated spirits enter the café
where you try and tell me things.
As if it mattered. My knowing still
expected like the silent breathing
of a house. I am lonely inside your
new voice, something about the miss
of touch. I am unsure of the nature
of hunger, love for satiation.
You go to the washroom and all I can
do is wonder if you'll come back, are
practicing how to expose your neck
to tempt my shy tongue, or if you
will start an argument.
Waiting, I smell the ghostly burn of a
woman, am covered by her violet
sheen. I see little but the beauty of
space, what it cannot hold for long
enough. And you slip, random, into a
nothingness I've tried to fill with urgent
moments; a choking heart that tries to
survive the feast of your desire. And
when I watch you at the counter,
ordering coffee, I think of ghosts like
bees, the torrid scent of honey and for
fear of never tasting you,

I don't dare run.

Glitter and Waste

I made a gesture over lunch you understood
as conversion,
the pull of trust; I am a woman who loves water.
In a rush of
cloth, my aquamarine dress shy and wrung by
your hand.

A social conjuror in Little Italy with fast fingers
fumbling for pussy
magic and martini talk to get you through my lies.
I murmur,
our beginning, baby, is not when we are born.

Later, wafting along College Street, you understood
that the sun is
best when broken by a breeze, that we mistook
fascination for
love, and are all out of sex.

On this side of the sun, baby, we are floating
glitter and waste.

Chance Operations

I

In the bar, conversation loiters, and you
won't admit you're tired of me. I can tell
you'd love to stitch my mouth shut. That
you don't listen to your own voice when
it breaks out of your throat, needy and
anxious. You're sick of me anaesthetizing
our past, dissecting how we've wasted
time remembering what we've lost. You
want me sorry for understanding your
sadness; that it's hard to feel good when
you live on amphetamine dreams that make
you cry headaches. You want me sorry,
but like all chance operations, it's too
early to tell if you'll fully recover, if I can
be held morally responsible or when you'll
feel safe from judgment.

II

I scalpel reason and turn you inside out.
We wear our faux fur skin to dinner or to
play pool and will always feel this cold on
one another, despite my accurate prognosis
and your successful transfusion.

Smoking is Sexy

I watch you smoke,
in love with its grey coolness,
uninterested reach.

Your fingers too, are lit,
the only fire you'll take in
your mouth.

Disarmed by green bar-light,
I inhale your exhale, say *sexy*
too late and you stay stuck in

my throat.

Ballad for a Bartender at the Rivoli

You are tired as you gaze out a second-
storey window. Hating me sitting here, as

if you could know I laced my way to find you,
up a purple cobwebbed stairwell, Friday night.

I rest and wait, shift my legs, latticework of velvet
and thread, I am *a bit of gold and braid.* Your

good looks sting like Caesar salt against my
lemon-wedged lips. I picture you

orientalizing my bed, tousled and lanky, my
warden. It's the Club Ravena T-shirt

and chains. I notice you notice I am noticing that
you are stark and timeless behind the bar, all beer

and distance, lime and cherry. I hold my glass like
a music box, a careful and common girl. Bet you've

seen me before and all my trained, stylish equivalents.
And I spy my failure with you in the twitching ice cubes

and movement of voices. *Oh, surrender,* I think as I
adjust my nails in my thighs, but you just crack another

Bud and water down another Coke... *we're caught in
a trap, I can't walk out, because I love you too much*

baby, why can't you see, what you're doin' to me...

You are made mostly of water, the calmness of a river,
waves cascading cold in my rocked heart. I play at

collapsing, divining a collision between us, but can only
wonder how you flourish. Long nights, ennui, women like

me who spin around you, art.

Isis, 925.13.42, Roman Gallery, ROM

I am not a restorative lover.

I cannot lift the burden of
guilt.

I am not a lover with heat.

I am not a lover of lettered
fragments; partial truths.

I am not a lover who smiles.

I smell like a museum.

American Windows

In room 1223, the fire
escape window is
propped by a phone
directory, and the smell
of indiscriminate lovers
stifles the room. Joggers
drill Ontario St., inter-
lock and break apart as
construction cracks this
8 a.m. in the middle and
coffee sorts me out. I read
framed newspapers
covering water-
stained walls: *The
President is killed* and get
a history lesson. TV
reporters discuss Kosovar
refugees, point at facts like
diaper rash and boredom. A
Texan woman says caffeine
is a godsend and I tip my
imaginary hat to her,
feeling spread in cream and
sugar, every brain cell full.
Skyscrapers encroach old
architecture with every sip,
the Davids and Goliaths of
Chicago, business and homeless
men exchange bargaining rules
while noise from the CTA rattles
the wooden tracks and me

inside, industry a stump of
underground grandeur, women
smoking on the platforms,
careless with their hands.
There is no quiet waking
here, music pumps a
different legend on every
corner. And in the Art
Institute I dive in Chagall's
glass and float beyond
these parallel lines,
looking out American
windows and drinking from a
bottomless cup.

Male Figure Reclining

He taught me to live in fire, he threw me there,
and then abandoned me on steppes of ice
                                    —*Marina Tsvetayeva*

He has clever hands, cruel eyes
because they are vacant and a
scar I would love to cross.

I play him like a composition and
don't pay well for a model. There
is little give to what I give.

I praise his marble torso, my
artistic habit. He exists primarily
of what abandons me: with each

exhale, I burn a little less. I want
to join him in the unfinished
study, but can't find a reason to

leave my place on the other side
of art. Clearly I am a liar, trying to
fit within the captured stillness of

his likeness. Aching with myth, the
sculpted linger of his gaze, I fumble
toward the marble's release.

And just before he lets me down,
because you will let me down,
I damn his hard kiss.

We are at carnival and I am in chartreuse

We are at carnival and I am in chartreuse,
the colour of kings. With an enchanted mouth
I stumble toward the funhouse mirrors: Allison

and Kim embarrass me by being beautiful.
Impatient, I let the body lead and there is every
cause for falling; in the vertical glass they are

sculpted stars I catch only a glimpse of. And
vanquished by the white of their reflections, a
dark fear waits but it is my own. Still and

shadowed in concave loveliness, I covet their
faces; and every potential sound that is cranked out
(screams from rollercoasters and my quiet cries)

is muffled with their laughter.

Malabar

On this old stage we played terrible
games. Fortune rattled, speech broke.

It was October when I foolishly followed
you to Malabar, its stone entrance.

Under the cupola we took shots of
tequila and you auditioned my laugh,

said it was baroque, all vampire teeth.
I knew you like a fox with a craft for

charm that unfurled, taught me to
suspect all black eyes. But I couldn't

knock my heels three times or read
between our scripted lines. And with

your good direction, I dramatized love
out of the clamour of rehearsed pillow

talk. You grew appropriately bored and
abandoned our show at my climax, a

vaudevillian exit. *It's just like you, Volpone,*
I called, tweaking my tail with pride,

making quick on a plastic broomstick, the
gold fluff of the curtain, my cape. You

left your snarling heart carelessly like a
scarf in the dressing room, you were too

young. I defended my fall for you: it was
in my nature and I was never a good

student. This old stage tired all your
reasons, these terrible games. You

tricked and I treated. But there is
change in wind, October.

At the Anne Frankhuis

She is a locked artifact: I read her family's death notices,
deportation cards and hear rails screeching, feel iron nails
at my neck. I want to press the fabric star of David to my
chest with its yellow thread that sticks out from the stitches,
an end to pull. Dad gently pushes me through, though the
sign reads "No Jews Allowed" in Dutch. But I am standing
in a long line of visitors and I know they can all see me,
here in her room, a shuffle of feet, tourist eyes. The walls
are glossy with glue over the faces of Shirley Temple,
Princesses Elizabeth and Margaret. I trip over Dad's whisper
and the line moves, comes to a document display; a list for
Auschwitz-Birkenau: WEISZ...
As a child would, I point at its boldness; I have always loved
discovering my name till now. Without breath I say *Daddy,
Daddy it's our name* and he looks at it with red, swollen eyes:
it's our name. And the name of hundreds of others. I find her
name clinging to these walls on Prinsengracht 263 and I too,
cling.

Auvers-sur-Oise, June 1890

after Vincent Van Gogh

The fields have been cultivated and
by late morning the farmer's work will be done.
I will sit here in this open, unspectacular space,
picture crows and take in the pulse of a working
day's light. I won't know what this ground will come to,
109 years after me, but fiery paint.

I will walk around, or perhaps through the
cemetery today. I will court the dead, say *hello* and
wish them well, even envy them in their silence.
I will be dwarfed by crosses rising like soldiers,
and I will learn to stand, awkward with the white sun,
in front of my name.

Night Healers

On a highway of goldenrod,
midnight is an escape route;

what remains is the fear the
chains might loosen and she'd

breathe. No experience
required, though the city is dull

with electricity, night healers.
She drives into its cure,

crowded with 2 a.m. ghosts
beckoning with want,

needles of a calmer dust.
Where apprehension passes

to rest and she exits with
everything she's got,

and nothing.

Notes

I know how furiously your heart is beating. Wallace Stevens from "Gray Room," in *Art & Love*, p.60.

Page 13: *in the days when we went gipsying, a long time ago.* Charlotte Brontë. *Jane Eyre.*

Page 16: *I shall never get you put together entirely,/ Pieced, glued, and properly jointed.* Sylvia Plath from "The Colossus," in *Contemporary American Poetry*, p.381.

Page 18: *All things are artificiall, for Nature is the Art of God.* Sir Thomas Browne, *Religio Medici*, 1643 (excerpted from *Baroque* by John Rupert, p.39).

Page 30: *the steep and thorny way to heaven.* Shakespeare. *Hamlet.* Act I.iii, l.48.

Page 37: *in my heat you disappear where you are.* The Book of Job, 6:17b. *Tanakh, The Holy Scriptures.*

Page 44: *a bit of gold and braid.* Stevie Nicks, lyric from "Gold and Braid," 1998.

Page 44-5: *we're caught in a trap / I can't walk out / Because I love you too much baby. Why can't you see / what you're doin' to me...* Mark James, lyric from "Suspicious Minds," 1956.

Page 49: *He taught me to live in fire, he threw me there, and then abandoned me on steppes of ice.* Marina Tsvetayeva from "Yesterday He Still Looked In My Eyes," in *Art & Love*, p.104.

Previously Published

"Stay," *Beneath the Surface*, spring 1997.

"Itinerant," *Algonquin Square Table Anthology*, 1999.

"Scar," Junction Books/Broadside, 1999.

"Malabar," *Green's Magazine*, fall 2000.

"Night Healers," "Subterranean," "We are at carnival and I am in charteuse," appeared online at *www.shenetworks.com,* August–September, 2000.